My Mother the Seal

My Mother the Seal

by ELIZABETH TREW

Published in 2023 by Hands-On Books
Cape Town, South Africa
www.modjajibooks.co.za
© Elizabeth Trew
Elizabeth Trew has asserted her right to be identified as the author of this work.

All rights reserved.

No part of this book may be reproduced or transmitted in any form or by any means, mechanical or electronic, including photocopying or recording, or be stored in any information storage or retrieval system without permission from the publisher.

Edited by Arja Salafranca
Cover artwork by Colleen Crawford-Cousins
Cover design by Monique Cleghorn
Book layout by Andy Thesen
Set in Georgia

ISBN print: 978-1-991240-15-6
ISBN e-book: 978-1-991240-16-3

For Kai and Leo

Contents

I	1
My mother the seal	3
The widows' house	4
A Norway tree	6
Fish	8
My grandmothers' hands	9
Kristina	10
Homecoming	11
Freedom	12
II	13
Four brides	15
Nativity	17
Strandfontein baby	18
Burrow	19
Convent meal	20
A farm story	22
Woman watching the sea	23
Shrine	25
The bright hair clasp	26
Theatre of hearts	27
Princess Vlei	28
Red disas	29
Shelter girls' outing	30
The messenger	31
The land recalls	32
Musi's donga	33

III 35

- The rat house 37
- The termite queen 38
- Cave 40
- Lighthouse 43
- Good morning, hadedas 44
- The Laughing Dove 45

IV 47

- The unknown valley 49
- Scaffolding 50
- The man from Darfur 51
- Neighbourhood watch 52

V 53

- The artist's house 55
- Madame Matisse 56
- Oranges 57
- The other shore 58
- Leavings 59
- Your melody 61
- Night busker 62
- Handwriting 63
- The prisoner 64
- Letters from Luvuyo 65
- Two lockdown days 66
- When you are a poem 68

Acknowledgements 69

I

My mother the seal

She felt at home in the sea
loving the warm waves of the Indian ocean,
even more the icy currents of the stormy Atlantic,
and the calm, oily waters of the harbour
between the ships where she met my father;
as a maid-seal she'd breast the width of Table Bay
before it became the foreshore filled with land,
sleekly rolling
flipping her long body
through the sea, her gentle dog face and eyes
ever watchful for sharks along our coastline
and offshore towards Robben Island.

She felt uncomfortable on land,
her shuffled walk slow, on painful
splayed feet thrust into shoes that didn't fit.
She'd walk with head bent
looking down at the ground.
When she sat behind the wheel of her car
we'd laugh at her slowness,
crawling along Main Road at twenty an hour
with streams of traffic in her wake.

Once as a pup I waited with her
at the harbour for my father's ship to come in
when she wept hot, seal tears into the sea.

The widows' house

In grandmother's high-pitched refuge
facing the train to the sea

she was Mom the new widow whose husband drank
she was her girl, the *laat lammetjie* brat
she was Aunt Alice, the widow of war
she was Aunt Lucy, whose husband was shot
she was Sylvia, the girl at the back
she was Grandmother, who kept fowls in a *hok*

he was the son away in the force
he was from hardware who came for the doors
he was the slave from the island, the maiden route
he was the man who courted the maid
he was a pair of trousers rolled in a bag
he was the stranger who sometimes called

Loquat and guava spin round the house,
Sylvia beats a rug on the washing line,
I turn cartwheels on grass.

Is that you, Sylvia?
Grandmother's voice reaches the dark.
Her room is airy and light. Here her polished bible,
her tablets of river-stones, containers of rain.
Sylvia lets down the old woman's white hair,
lets out her whalebone waist.
Kleingeluk! *Spinnekop*! cries the Snow Queen
practising her Afrikaans.
Sylvia comes with polishing cloths,
shines silver and brass
to flick heaviness out the house.

We are Silvo and Brasso doing the cross-over duo.
Dream lover! she croons, rolling limbo hips
to my waspish dance.

Aunt Alice treads heavily down the passage
past her husband's framed regiment.
On the stoep, Grandmother sings to Sylvia
in her cracked staccato. She winds in loops of wool
which Sylvia holds out.

Sylvia serves us at the widows' table
where we eat in silence off willow plates.
She drinks from her *sweetmilk* tin kept under the sink.

She plasters her walls with magazine cuttings,
newspaper fills her window crack.
She is meeting Henry by the fowl *hok*,
throws off her cap to shake out black hair
and shine on sweet grease. Glitter shoes
and flowering earrings. *Hey-O—ready to go!*
A psychedelic rainbow that clicks the gate shut.

In my room at the front, I hear voices ghosting at night,
the click-switch outside of the signal box,
the wheels of the train when the windows shake,
the conductor's last whistle and shout.

A Norway tree

On the way to my father's tundra place
far north of the southern Cape,
I sat in a wooden prow
in my scarlet riding coat.
I sailed along the deepest fjord
by the mossy feet of the precipice.
Tree-roots clung to ice-scarred rock
and branches floated past.
High above, a herd of reindeer
crossed the snow.
All left their long reflections in the boat
on the glassy sea below.

Along wide water, rich fishing grounds,
and fertile banks of peach and plum,
where folded grass hung out to dry.
By their inlet sea all my north kin
leaned out to me.
I clutched the leaves of my other tongue
as Johanna shyly showed me in.
A feast of fish and bread was laid
on the rose embroidery, and
on wooden walls all the faces of my solemn kin.
That night I tossed in a wooden cot
in the tail of the midnight sun.

They came to meet his youngest child, and
told me the tale of Olaf's son with the golden eye
who, long ago, had sailed away
to Africa's southern Cape
while the village church bells rang.
Everywhere my father's face,

on every table meals of fish and bread, and
in the darkest evergreen
soft falling trees,
the piercing grind of someone sawing wood
as I heard my father's factory saw-mill
in the valley at the Cape.

Once we reached the fjord's snout
Alfred, in his dark-blue Sunday suit,
pushed out his boat to grandmother's place
on the other mountain side.
He rowed across with a plash of oars
facing me in my bright red coat
as I trailed my hand in milk-blue waves
brushing the little fishing boat.

Alfred rowed to the lapping edge.
We walked past folded hay and
my father's hut.
Along the path, a blond horse cropped the grass,
crows flew to the trees. I ran to her and
saw my startled face in hers.
Farmor* sat in her heavy shawl,
her long hair knotted and tied.
Many times she cried out,
clasped me, daughter of her long-lost son.
*Velkommen, Olafsdatter, kom!**

---

farmor – Norwegian for paternal grandmother

Velkommen, Olafsdatter, kom – Norwegian for 'Welcome Olaf's daughter, come!'

Fish

With a trace of Grandfather's eyebrows, like fish-
bones, we'd watch jars of goldfish and angel fish

joined by a brother, we'd make arms of a starfish
drawn to the silver fish darting in rock pools

beside me, two chubby boys baiting their strings
over the pond, hooked in their first bite

learned to spear sand-shark basking in shallows
rafted brown river mouths and blue waves wielding rods

my lean fish-boys grown anglers, rowed out
casting nets overnight, these Vikings in longboats

as I balanced on rock the pull lengthened between us
our histories flapping, they hauled in their catch

in their net primal hagfish—sinuous greys
dredged from the deeps—fish of the rainbow

My grandmothers' hands

Grandma Helen's hands were soft and white
spotted brown from the African sun,
hands made to crochet long coloured strips
she'd stitch together for family beds,
hands to carry her work-bag of wool,
hands to smooth huge feathered hats
and play an upright piano.
She'd sit at the foot of my bed plying her wool
with her crochet hook and sharply sing
her favourite song to me:
Count your blessings!
Count them one by one.

Farmor* Karen's hands were strong and red
used to shovelling Nordic snow,
hands to tend rows of raspberry canes,
hands to dig, plant and harvest potatoes,
hands to bake bread, light fires,
feed the pig and hold a farmer's crook
to drive sheep up to their summer pasture.
Hands that tied her headscarf tight.
On a visit to the family farm
I placed fresh flowers upon her grave
and ceremoniously watered them.
Family say I am like her.

* Norwegian for paternal grandmother

Kristina

My aunt spoke loudly in her Nordic lilt—
louder when she was on the phone,
yet louder and slower when
she spoke to me.

She was dark stockings and boots
that strode down the hill
and knelt among sheep.
She was mended fishing nets.

We'd sit in summer under trees
with a jug of home-made juice.
Inside her house she looked long
through glass at the waterfall
across the fjord.
Today he is big and strong, or
Today he flows softer than before.

She was the steady gaze and force
of falling water,
a keeper of nets and sheep
and new-laid eggs.
She was mid-summer bonfires along the fjord,
the stamp of boots that
carried wood for the indoor fire.
She was hearty soups and stews
from her steamy kitchen,
calling me to lay the table.
Come eat! Be big and strong.

Homecoming

I walk through cones of primrose light
turning my life's web on London grass
by sheds of water flowing into the drowned canal.
I find you in the river's bow
stringing flags to welcome me.
On the bridge you
pass me by on roller blades
turning shoes with tiny keys.
On the stairs you brush my coat with lemon stars.
Sipping every voice of you
I drench my boots with snowdrop lids
let my litmus lift and turn the wheel
across our world,
my leaving you.

My exiled days return to you,
nudge my certain landing
rush towards your open cosmos eye
through gold-reef doorways city deep.
Under the bridge I touch your scars
and broken lips.
On the hill my trumpet vines
reveal the ruby blare of you.
I tap the mourning earth
replace my roots,
line my river paths with river feet
the spirit flow of you,
return my bedrock dance to you,
my coming home.

Freedom

Leaves a window open
lifts the latch
lets itself out

travels across borders
rides the tall wave
feels the furnace

pushes and struggles
cries and sheds blood
arrives shiny new

powers its own house
reaches and
holds unknown music

unfreezes its streams
looks afresh
at the face of another

Freedom broods, gives birth
in the blood of itself
is never alone.

II

Four brides

1
A shy bride, and groom and family procession
glide through gates of a public garden.
Fresh lilies to her breast
small hooks and eyes down her back
her net opens as sisters and mothers lift the veil
trawling a heavy sloop of sun,
the men pushing back
swags of shed bark and wild fruiting bananas.
She takes small dancer steps beside
his bobbing Adam's apple
between nodding agapanthus,
along avenues of avocados,
rubber trees and rose apples
while butterfly children burst out of their seams
licking ice-cream melting in dust.
Her sisters encircling
splash peach and lime dresses onto the grass.
Many hands lay out the wide skirt.
Hands turn her head to his tight, frilling chest.

2
On a river barge sending
out streamers away from its quay
a bride and groom march
through the applause of a thundering banquet.
She turns in her peacock-blue suit,
emerald bag under her arm,
her net reaching the rim of an eye.
Hooked cabin lamps burn as he opens a cake
to read messages soaked in his blood,
turns to his bride putting candy to tongue,

peels off his jacket and shakes to the rhythm
of his wild floral waistcoat.
Out of an eye her groom dances and sings.

3
The professor of Japanese art glows with happiness.
His bride blushes and bows to the circle of eyes.
Her ginkgo-leaf kimono flutters to the murmur of strangers.
No one, not even the groom, can speak Japanese.

4
Evening shadows his manicured lawn
as she moves from his old candelabra,
flies over the steps among guests
milling silver and pearl
knotting the green.

He holds out a tray of cold meat
eyeing her children.
Deftly she brushes past shoulders,
runs fingers through his hair,
around his tie, into his pocket,
her long lilac sleeves folding wave
after wave onto darkening green.
Old bride, her pearls spooling as a white
cake is wheeled out, soap-smooth and clean.

Nativity

Pink hibiscus wide as plates outside Holiday Inn
we bring bangles and mats, many coloured bead chains
for wrist, ankle and neck—
blue-green of sea, red-brown of ground.

We thread beads in our laps sitting on soft water grass
know hunger and death,
speak of men and youth gone
drilling oil along coasts, gold far away.

Venus serves the white godfathers, high in this place.
Maak gou, Venus, the chef says.
She is big like a beach-ball, like the full moon,
soon her waters will break.

We go small, we go light, heads high with cloth,
beads to breast, robes to ground
we bring blankets and mats
and buchu for birth.

Strandfontein baby

for Niamaat

i
Friends, an extraordinary story:
while walking with my sister along
the beach we saw something in the surf—
a plastic supermarket bag, strange
and swollen. Imagine our shock
when we opened it and pulled out a baby—
Alive! Smeared with blood and afterbirth,
the navel cord still attached.
He was meant to drown
but the waves brought him back.

ii
They tell me I was reborn in the sea—
found in the waves by two sisters.
They opened my second womb,
in the breaking waters they delivered me.
I bear the blood of the sea
and my birth mother's darkness.
I watch the moon's sheen on the ocean
drawn to her incoming waves.
Alone in my silence I am slowly learning
to love my dark days.

Burrow

Finding Emi

She says goodbye, kisses her baby
into the care of her sister.
She wants to walk on the mountain
above the running ocean.

The earth hears her among rocks and scrub
till she falls headlong into an animal burrow.
The sky closes in.

All day she hears calling voices.
The wind howls, drowns out sound.
Runners' feet pound and fade.
The sky darkens.

Darkness settles.
She weeps the wild night.
Daylight comes, the rescue helicopter

sweeps the sky.
Her body is found curled in her den
anchored by roots and stones:
the earth her pillow.

Convent meal

Today
Mother Superior
presides at high table.
Solid in habitual black
she graces the food,
sits and eyes
tranquilly
whorls of girls
in drifting blue—tender
petals of profusion whose
transient faces
hover above the brisket,
eddying high sound
as the water-jug passes

while she,
over bread pudding
ever smiling
enquiring
sinks teeth, smooth ivory notes
vigorously
into the sweet.

Later
we all rise to more prayer
the girls dispersing into hazy sky
of their outside court
flying fine hair and bones
between the bells

while she,
highest Mother of the house
swings heavy robes through
hallowed corridors:
perpetually.

A farm story

Kept with care on the sisters' dairy farm:
two giant eucalypts—
beloved and long dead
stand beside the old house.
I arrive at dusk.
Bees are busy making honey
inside a dead trunk,
Kei apples, fallen, lie under their trees,
guinea fowl fly into the pines to sleep,
calves gambol in the field.
All so very beautiful, one sister says to me
taking me through the house
of many ageing things, so very quietly kept.
An old wedding dress hangs inside my room.
I open a tin of hairpins belonging to the bride,
lie awake between the living and the dead,
hear the windmill turn and creak,
the bone-white trees
and wedding dress
loom inside the night.

Woman watching the sea

Stonetown, Zanzibar

Bound to the inner court of my master's house
tied to silver drops of my lady's bath
I climb wooden steps with scented cloths
and bow to the breeze and coconut.

On the roof he carves tendrils
of flower and leaf on each ebony bed
while I sit cross-legged on my mat,
my tongs chipping the sugar block.
Below I hear boat-builders hammering
the dhow's pliant mango wood.

Always a memory. Kept in the female chamber
below stone as low as my lady's canopy bed
down to the groans of our teeming air,
in my mother's arms, inhaling her breath,
watching the hole where sea rushes in
too small to crawl through,
then pushed out to cutlass light
held at the trader's whipping post
where my mother fell and I was bought.

Last night in my sleep
I dreamed of him carving our bed.
I tunnelled and climbed through velvet folds
up tassel ropes
cleaving the wind out the merchant's house.
Today I sit on stone watching the sea,
think of those on the island.

*

Island prison abandoned—stone heart cast in the sea
last stop for slaves—runaways

wind sweeps the trees
a peacock's feather and tortoise shell

falls to a hush in a cavity of cells
a seed left on a broken wall

anchors a small fig and throws aerial roots
down to inhabit the prison

roots dig galleries of earth below stone
above manacles lashed to the whipping pit

branches weave a harp around
milk-soft leaves and blood-red fruit

look seaward to the landing rock
in a desperate embrace

Shrine

In the heart of your home,
is the Japanese room
where I enter barefoot,
bow and clap on the tatami mat
before a face smiling out of the frame—
beloved husband and father

his portrait centred inside a gold shrine
between candles and offerings:
water in a jar, fresh flowers in glass,
a tin of keepsakes
and our gifts from Africa
still to be opened

laughter from the grandsons we share
coming from the room next door.

The bright hair clasp

Painting by Suma Maruki

The old painter's face is
delicate and gentle; her furrows
of years have a look of repose,
her mouth compressed in sorrow—
illiterate peasant woman who survived
the terrors of Hiroshima and found Art.

Her painting flashes open—
a so-called primitive set in a garden
melancholy and dreaming
filled with an assembly of companions—
snakes, chickens, ducks, songbirds
among miraculous trees
painted in countless variations
of greeny blues, smoky pinks
and lilacs with bold touches of mustard:

all bolted and clasped through her hair
like lightning.

Theatre of hearts

Hamilton Naki, 1926–2005

Remember Hamilton
who rose from gardener
to cleaner of animal cages
to teacher-with-no-training of students and physicians
to black laboratory assistant of Christiaan,
the white heart surgeon:
Technically, Hamilton is a better surgeon than I am.
Some operations I cannot do.

Confined to a back room
he removes, inserts and stitches livers
jugulars and hearts into the flesh of a giraffe
and many dogs and pigs:
Animals Only.

See him cross the courtyard of Groote Schuur.
He carries a box of hearts for his surgeon
and enters a lift:
Non-Whites Only.

Today in the Christiaan Barnard Hospital
a girl in the ward of damaged hearts calls:
Mammy! Mammy!
and I listen to the voice
of the black doctor
back from theatre
moving bed to bed on his rounds
to hear each desolate
human heart.

Princess Vlei

Here opening the valley
the eye of a princess
her fertile tear hemmed in a watershed

Here tasting salt bending
daughter-streams drink

Here her bruised mouth
where the stubbled marsh grows

Here from her throat bending
daughter-streams drink

Here milk and blood mingle

Here her smoke drifts
kissing wattle and willow

Here waiting still is the voice of the water maid,
maker of smoke, and dew

Red disas

Mountain pride, the brown butterfly
spies flaring reds
beside the dark water,
demure virgins of the dance hall
waiting in flared skirts
for a partner.
He lands lightly on a petal
unrolling his tongue
to sip her nectar
while she douses him
with a yellow shower
before he goes on
from flower to flower,
filling his sacs with pollen,
putting out each fire.

Shelter girls' outing

The aunties took us out to a *beautiful* garden.
We ate hot dogs and apples under a tree.
A big bird wanted my food.
Voetsek! I shouted. He hissed but went away.
Egyptian goose, said auntie Anne.

Twenty girls under the oak:
not Asanda—unwell, with nurse at home
not Gloria, the new girl—unwell, raped by her uncle
not Sibongile—ran away with her baby to boyfriend

Out and fancy-free! says auntie Queen.
Thandi, Mercy, Michele and me up and down
and around the flower-beds meeting people.

Two ladies from Korea overseas were laughing at us.
They let us touch their skin and hair—skin like cream
and real hair, straight and black.

We played by a pool made like a bird—
Mr Bird's bath. *Sorry auntie*, I said when
she saw us throw little stones in.

We climbed the almond tree that the Dutch settler
van Riebeeck planted to keep people like us
out of his property.

not the abandoned girl
not the missing girl
not the beaten girl

The messenger

Mind the sprinklers spinning
inside the scorched garden.
Go up the steps. As her guard dogs
leap out unbolted
they kiss me nearly knock me over

Reach out a greeting
as I go down the dark passage,
her big shaded home
mindful of love between mother
and banished, barred son.

Attend as the messenger
who brings shiny bags filled with news.
As her hand presses lightly, retelling
the flight into exile, leafing through cuttings
and snapshots curled yellow.

Pink flowers sway browning
beneath her barred sill,
raw meat hangs on hooks
above creamy pitchers of milk.
Inside the cool kitchen
the roast lies on starched cloth.

Going out the steps linger,
tear the flecked path.
As her hand burns her blue necklace
go take her picture
by the palm-tree he planted.
Go with love.
Go.

The land recalls

Luyolo village, Simonstown, 1896–1965

The land recalls
                a wounded history—
families uprooted in the kloof
                above Long Beach,
their village removed by force ...

calls inside rows of small houses
                doors open to the sea,
singers at weddings, in church
                and primary school,
murmurs of workers returning at dusk.

Gale-force winds whistle and keen,
                snatch my hat
in an overcast sky
                I scramble up rock
lodged in sand between bush
                and burnt trees.

Nothing of church, school or house
                on the empty terraces
but buried in sand a child's shoe,
old bottles and spoons,
buttons and bullets.

High on the slope a splash of new red—
a candelabra in flower,
rooted in sand.

Musi's donga

in memoriam Fanuel Musi

Laid in your donga of earth
stones and soil fill your mouth.
I sit by thatching grass
in our boundary of poplars and ash
sisal each side of the village path
with our two willows—the basket and weeping
between mealies and beans, almond and peach.

When the storm raged, ripping up ground
rains beating, floods churning
sweeping down soils
you wept on the hill in two dongas cut deep
broken mouths—empty hearts.

Sixteen summers bowed across dongas
lifting your apron full of stones
collecting stones—carting stones
channelling rain—stemming rain
collecting silt—cradling silt
bridging and earthing

autumns, winters gathering and rooting
gentling dung and ash in
swarding grass in
tilling seeds in
releasing—piping the spring.

Days taking bread and tea down
working sweet passion on.
Nights rubbing in aloe jelly

washing calluses and cuts
washing coloured soils and Lesotho dust.

Soft in this earth
stones and soil fill your mouth.
I sit in my harvest dress
red bishops trill in the thatching grass,
your heart in your donga of earth
and in mine.

III

The rat house

She was constantly mothering,
enclosed in her house nursing Harm.

Did that whiskery gentleman
unbutton his tweeds, his breath
on her neck, his body filling her house?

Did her body swell, tiny feet
kicking to come out, soon to give
multiple birth?

Soon she had her hands full
putting out bowls of warmed milk
and tenderised meats for her children

who ran amok in the lounge oiling the furniture
munching biscuits and flour in the kitchen
racing up and down passage and stairs

stillborns kept in a jar
newborns asleep in a drawer
the two who played in a shoe

When they took her out pleading,
My babies, don't take them away!
I could finally meet her.

The termite queen

i
Dusk, after rain, I crawl from the nest
needing to fly, become a flying queen
before I dismantle my wings and wait for a king.
Our honeymoon flight—frantic through dark
between owls and hawks as we search for a home
before I breed the community.

My antennae sweep and circle my palace chamber,
my jaws work through pain—
deep contractions for birth.
I lie stroking my children
before they are taken to the nursery.

Bloated in my royal chamber
I birth thousands of babies each hour.
Within my republic, a host of passages
lead to food gardens and nurseries
kept moist and cool.
Workers roll grains of sand
to build and repair the inner sanctum,
feed me and my brood from a belly of fungus.
Bodyguards carry flasks of poison to protect me,
each organ tied to my power.

ii
He finds her under the floor in the darkest corner
of one room, her body swollen and trapped in
the palace cavity, the loyal king clambering over her.

Workers surround her—lift her head
to feed and carry away the multitude of eggs.

Her soldiers stand guard—some on the floor,
others upside down on the roof pointing north
towards earth's magnetic pull
all swaying their hypnotic dance around their queen.

The task nearly done, his workmen
remove the breeding gardens in other rooms
while he captures the queen.
Without her, the composite termite body
collapses and dies.

Cave

1 Tartarus
for Alet

We bend into Tartarus' mouth
holding flashlights,
descend the wet, winding cavern
between weeping rocks, rainpools.
I see the cave in ancient Greece,
Tantalus in that hellish abyss
tortured by demons and tempted by fruits
and sweet water he cannot reach.

Our cave is cold, empty, dark. We see
no bones, no signs of life. Then you cry
in fear, scramble back
as our passage deepens.
You see the boys in Thailand
trapped for days underground
in a chamber of rising floodwaters
that no one can reach.

Yet while I write and the world waits
each boy with his pilot to guide him
swims towards you,
through to the light.

2 Echo

Bordering the farm valley, I disappear
down a cavern of echoes—

like the shepherd
who found an underground refuge
and drummed an icicle tooth
to warn his tribe;
or the farmer
who found the shepherd's clay pot.

Inside the slippery jaws of the crocodile
I squeeze between drip-stone teeth,
tread clay seeping river-fat
where porcupines sleep.

In the burial chamber
I drum a crocodile's tooth
like the shepherd whose echo
once warned his tribe.

A Madonna appears crystal white,
bows her head as I pass.
She cries seaweed tears
for her child never found never found.

3 Cango

Behind the San's shelter, the shepherd's entry,
the farmer's tunnel of dreams,
we join the throng beside rainbow-lit drip-stones
and a citrus Madonna who burns under neon.

Behind a lime-stone curtain we crawl
through the tunnel of love to the palace garden
where blind white insects inhabit their darkness.

As our feather-breath dissolves
great Cango shrinks.

Lighthouse

I missed the moon last night
but saw the lighthouse cast a guardian eye
over the coast.
Today a child climbs the tower and waves
to her mother below.
Inside I see maps of Africa
from the Portuguese mariner
beside Khoisan fish traps
and a tree festering flip-flops
plastic bags, fish lines and more
fetched from the shore.

I walk towards ocean, place a stone
onto another and advance to the rocks—
jagged limestone—graveyard of ships
drowned sailors, fishermen,
children swept away by tides,
inhale its breath where two currents meet—
warm and cold mingle
with an unknown third in flux.

Seaweed at my feet, an old mole-snake
rises from its rocky den.
Guard of the rocks he pauses inside my shadow,
flicks a forked tongue, gleams a wise eye
then ripples away.

Good morning, hadedas

Cloud has come down
over Lion's Head,
almost to my gate.
Children in their class
across the road
chant high and sweet:
The farmer takes a wife!
The farmer takes a wife!

Two courting hadedas
rustle near the path
with clacking beaks
and courtship purrs.
Good morning, hadedas.
Good morning, hadedas.

I brush past
the gooseberry bush
with a pile of papers,
the news of the world
ready to be dumped
and then recycled.

The Laughing Dove

the smallest dove
nests among new
leaves of my vine

turns slowly clockwise
nudging her warmth
around her careful egg

folds her wings
turns her cinnamon back
her white-tip tail

keeps all ways
the growing embryo
against her breast

unshaken by the howling gale
the piercing drill next door
or the glare of my outside light

IV

The unknown valley

A pale girl in dark despair
lives in a vale of health

I cannot find the red gods of her valley
as the valley of angels

becomes the valley of ghosts.
Beneath it, the city of Atlantis

lies in the sea
and the city bowl hides in a forest of cloud.

One place I can trust is the marsh of sleep
on the pock-marked moon.

Scaffolding

1
Builders on platforms and ladders replace
pipes, walls, floors, ceilings and doors
of his broken house.

2
He collects sheets of cardboard, iron,
tin, plastic and planks to make
a temporary shelter of home.

3
She props herself onto pillows,
faces a cloud of darkness
her wild arms beating it away.

4
He lies trembling in the road,
his body lifted carefully onto a stretcher
young neck held in a brace.

5
She puts a drooping daffodil in a cup of water,
gentles a rubber splint around its stem
and secures it to her cup.

6
Gardeners in the park revive an old buckled tree,
wheedle and coax it upright with ropes
pulleys and poles. The old tree persists.

The man from Darfur

comes to my door most days of the year
for any small thing—some food or coins
for his wife and baby to stay at The Haven.
Some days I give bread and peanut butter,
today a bag of avocados from my tree in season.

I know it's him by his ring of the bell.
I hand him small things through the fence
but don't know his name or how he came here.
Sometimes he's gone for weeks—
schizophrenia, then returns to my door,
this man of sorrow displaced from Darfur.

Today I come for the last time, Madame.
We leave today for Darfur. No peace here—
xenophobia. Today some food for the journey
please. I hand him a bag through the fence.
Weep for him, who came with such hope
and found a place of hate.

Neighbourhood watch

Down the block, past the guesthouse with fairy lights
Vusi smiles in his corner by the supermarket
beading royal-blue rhinos and red chilli key rings.

Peter, Old Soldier—tracker from a spent force
wears a tall hat and black winter coat, paints
rabbits, ducks and flowers he displays outside the church.

Good day, Mama, how are you? And the avocados?
The car-guard greets me politely from his wheelchair—
legs lost when stepping on a landmine in Mozambique.

The couple, who sleep in the bus shelter leave
before the first bus. Sometimes the man sits
in the park while his wife goes 'collecting'.

The man hungry to read comes to my door.
Thanks for the André Brink. Says he wants a bible.
My parents were burnt on a farm when I was three.

The vigilante up the road looks out for 'undesirables'
carries a gun and wears a bullet-proof vest.
He shakes his head at me.

V

The artist's house

He works with past lives gone
into silt, ash and resins. His talisman
a bee trapped in amber—
tears of the sun god Apollo.

Inside his frames he prints inky tadpoles,
fixes dragonfly wings to watercolours,
ferries into the ground floor fallen leaves
found in underbrush, patterns them like hands
against rubbled cities.
He singes and seals fallen leaf tones onto parchment,
plasters his walls with burnt olives and charcoals,
guttering nutmegs and cold copper leaves.

The apprentice upstairs opens tins—
powdered acrylics, intense coloured lights.
Into her pollens she mixes and stirs, adds
the sky's tones and borrows from the master
downstairs a handful of charcoals,
a few yellow tears.

Onto her walls she outlines her city,
paints with wide-shouldered brushes
the brilliance of reds, purples, blues.
Windows and doors boil with light.
Black eyes of her sunflowers shed eyelids.

She pours out her city's fluorescence
spilling through skylight
cascading downstairs,
launching her scripts on his coppery bed.

Madame Matisse

Mon Dieu! Matisse—master of colour ...
my fluttering fan and oval face
a riot of pinks and greens in *Woman with the Hat*.

I am dressed as a matador in *The Guitarist*.
He kicked his easel and ripped off my costume
as I wouldn't sit still. Later we laughed about that.

I sit demure, elegant in another hat
then I emerge as *Madame Matisse*,
a bold green line dividing my face.

Mostly he likes me in black and white
to balance his clashing explosions of colour
while I endured outbursts of another sort—
his doubting, weeping, violent self.

He began to paint nudes—vermillion dancers
and a *Blue Nude with Straw Hat*. A huge *Pink Nude*
almost falls in my lap.

He moved to the silvery light of Nice. I saw him less
and less. During the war I joined the Resistance
while he painted *Paradise* in his *appartement*

rearranging his voluptuous models and
nudes and tending his beloved birds:
the long black plumage of widow birds,
the blinding whiteness of doves.

Oranges

After 'Why I'm not a painter', by Frank O'Hara

Orange brings in the light—
>orangeade of the sun

orange lifts the spirit—
>orange fizzes my shirt

orange deepens at dusk

Oranjezicht—
place of oranges, where my friend paints her room
fiery orange.
At home I paint the chimney breast darker—
burnt orange.
I confess to have something of an orange crush and live
with my marmalade cat.
Sweet navels and Valencias wait on my table while the cat
watches me slice blood oranges.
I remember how my mother ate an orange—snip and sugar
then squeeze and suck juice from its teat.
Oh no! says my friend, after I've repainted the dark.
It was too much, I say.

Orange brings in the light
orange fires the spirit
orange darkens at dusk.

The other shore

Derek Walcott, 1930–2017

Brave New World poet
in a star-apple kingdom
the sea as history in your bones

you hear an ocean of leaves
drowning her children,
the crossing of slaves
on the hot iron ocean,
sounds of the cranked waterwheel
and its inheritors—trees of the island:
masts of women's hair
hanging from branches,
bodies of sea almonds fired
on the beach, enduring their grief,
mangroves slipping back to darkness.

You as the restless nomad
leaves the island to steer
between exile and home, your own
odyssey across oceans
city to Old World city—
the other shore before coming home
to St Lucia's light,
her firefly's little lamp.
A star-apple fallen your voice endures.

Leavings

Potter

She is crafting something new
out of the clay
on her potter's wheel—
some ghost of her past
curled into a ball

using water to soften
it ripples its skin in time

with the hum:
a small death of yesterday
taking residence today.

Mother

I remember your
meaty breath on my face
as you bent down with a kiss:
as I lean over to inhale
your last yeasty breaths
to savour, exhale, kiss the sky.

Child

The women consoled and held her.
I don't know where to be!
A mother cries out in shattered grief.
All she can see

are her tears in a leaden sky.
She will find somewhere
to pave her daughter's lyrical step
in the rustle of leaves
and sound of bells.

Painter

I will paint my old friend in sombre colours
lying on his bitter green robe of grass
with a harsh white cloth over his face.
And his rooster in radiant shades of cinnabar,
the earth brown, and the bluish-green
rhythm of hills gently receding.

Your melody

for Siphiwe ka Ngwenya

H e y! dark-bright poet-man
sugar-man rain-man

your melody
pounds the maize and shakes the pot

your melody
bounces on a shock wave
wakes up a battlement
knocks on a locked door
hums through a gold-chink
blows down a chain gang
taps in a blues-beat
drums on a rainpipe

your melody
spins by a lift shaft
calls from a highrise
to denizens of Hillbrow

melody to melody
memory to harmony
tuning words of liberty

tender torrentials
hot explosions of the soul
slow lullabies of love

Night busker

Dusk, rush hour, when
people pass under the city
a husky blues pedlar
who sings city solo
moves along
down
to her lupin-lit underground,
busking the bough
on her balcony of branches

along the lines
down
moves above the rap-rattle
to siren the shuttle,
drifting night riders and
rocking the bough

moves along
descends deeper
to stationless drifters—
late buds on the bough.

Handwriting

for Tony

They found you alive in the morgue,
scars on your tough, battered face
from your head-on crash

reset nose, cheekbone and jaw
stitched back your skin
your head held in place by a cage

Somebody swore at your face in the cage.
Go for plastic surgery, your mother begged

choosing instead a far country
to mend post office mailbags, alone.
A blackbird sang to me all summer long, you said

Back home sunburn imprinted on skin
mending mailbags in political prison

when I caught your first tear behind soundless glass
in the visitor's room, our country apart in a cage

Writing to me from your cell
I dreamed of your tear and your head

tough builder's hands, the flight of birds
song of your chest, sheen of your back

dovetailing raisin-sweet salt,
decades mending skin

The prisoner

A prisoner opens a smuggled, battered book
written by a girl concealed in her country,
a girl marked by a yellow star in hiding
writing to herself at an angle of the stairs
in a dark house, with words shining through the dark.
Quiet and still her breath mists the window crack
above yellow-starred people moving in the street.

Day 235: *I make my own stars patient and calm.*

Day 613: *I long to move freely under the stars.*

Monday evening, 8 November 1943:
I see eight of us hidden inside a piece of blue sky
surrounded by gathering darkness closing in
squeezing us more tightly
until we make our own star which cannot be crushed yet.

He collects the girl's days, writing her words
small on a paper scrap, which he rolls up tight,
hides on himself to be smuggled to others
until the bloom of her words fills each cell.

Note: *The Diary of Anne Frank* was passed around Robben Island.

Letters from Luvuyo

Found poems

1
Dear Liz

So sorry for taking your mirror.
The reason is that in my room I have no mirror
And I forgot to inform you about that.

2
Dear Liz

Please forgive me for taking your dictionary
without permission. I'm just using it.
And please can you fill the sentence below:
Do not count the chicken ...

Two lockdown days

Tuesday, June 16, 2020
Youth Day, the students' uprising,
refuse day, when the young collector
hoists my bag, dark eyes above his mask.

I prepare the room for yoga on Zoom.
Come on Liz, kick up quickly into Scorpion.
You have the strength, you know.

A day too sunny for indoors we walk
up Signal Hill, watch two friendly dogs
chase each other head to tail.

We speak to Michael locked in his quarantine hotel,
sun setting, fire crackling, warming our winter room.

Wednesday, June 17, 2020
I try to kick into the scorpion before breakfast, then
watch a masked mother and child enter the primary school

two cleaners in royal-blue overalls and white gumboots
sweep the empty playground, cordon the jungle gym.

I walk to High Places through deserted streets, workmen
inside a building site, three hadedas screaming in the sky

a lost dog runs into the closed German school,
I pass a dead rat, hear runner's feet behind me.

Up Quarry Hill I take in blue heaven, green mountain,
three ships outside the harbour waiting to dock

walking down, a flock of sparrows tweet in a tree.
No desperate calls at our gate tonight.

When you are a poem

you are the wild child at my knee
the fearless youth, ebullient and strong
the gentle fugitive who went away

the joyful prodigal who returns
the hungry traveller in flight
to feed your dreams

when you arrive barefoot at the door
for you gave your shoes
to a homeless man on the road

I wish you could see in your lonely dark
your own astonishing light *

* Hafiz of Shiraz (b. 1325)

Acknowledgements

With thanks to the following journals and anthologies where versions of some of these poems first appeared: *The Rialto, ISISx, New Coin, New Contrast, Scrutiny2, Carapace, Stanzas, McGregor Poetry Festival Anthology 2020 and 2021, Prodigal Daughters. Stories of South African Women in Exile*, edited by Lauretta Ngcobo.

I would like to thank:
Colleen Higgs for her insight;
Finuala Dowling for her inspiring poetry workshops, writing courses and mentoring;
Pleached Poets for the years of laughter during poetry mornings;
and Tony for being there.

In memory of Michael.

Photograph by: Tony Trew

Elizabeth Trew was born and grew up in Cape Town. She left South Africa and returned in 1991 after 27 years in exile in England. A former librarian and teacher in adult education in England and Johannesburg, she has an MA in English Education from Wits. Her poems have appeared in various poetry journals in UK and South Africa. She is a language editor and volunteers at a shelter for girls in Cape Town.

"The world is richer for having Liz Trew's sparse yet translucent poems published as a collection at last. Her work is simple yet powerful, tender and haunting. She sings with a pure clear sonority through the different registers of protest, lament and deep yearning for home, for bliss. Her wry humour delights and honours her ancestors."—**Liesl Jobson**

www.ingramcontent.com/pod-product-compliance
Lightning Source LLC
Chambersburg PA
CBHW070550090426
42735CB00013B/3139